Body of Starlight

Poems by

Melissa Carroll

Sweet Aperitifs
Tampa, FL
2019

Body of Starlight

Copyright © 2019 by Melissa Carroll
All rights reserved.
Printed in the United States

No part of this book may be reproduced, stored in a retrieval system, or transmitted in any form or by any means, eletronic, mechanical, photocopying, recording, or otherwise, except as may be expressly permitted by the applicable copyright statutes or in writing by the publisher.

Sweet Aperitifs
Tampa, Florida
Cover Photo by: Luiz Clas
Author Photo by: Gordon Tarpley
Epilogue Illustrations by: Lauren Chidelww
Cover and Book Design by: J.R. Miller
The text of this book is set in Garamond

ISBN 978-0-9848681-8-6

Acknowledgments

Grateful acknowledgement is made to the following publications in which some of these poems appeared, some in slightly different versions:

Ascent Aspirations: "String Theory"

Blood Lotus Journal: "Panning for Stars"

Creative Pinellas Magazine: "How to Cook Like an Italian Woman," "Beware the Poem with Wine Stain," & "The Merits of Failure"

Greatest Uncommon Denominator: "7 Ways to Fake an Orgasm"

The Literary Bohemian: "Cantina"

MEAD: A Journal of Literature & Libations: "Your Orgasm as a Veritable Carmen Sandiego (I)" (Originally published under the title "How to Hunt Down Your Orgasm")

Poetry Quarterly: "I Love the Girls"

Waterhouse Review: "Straight to Hell"

About The Author

Melissa Carroll is a poet, writer, and yoga teacher based in Tampa Bay. She is the editor of the essay collection *Going OM: Real-Life Stories on and off the Yoga Mat* (Viva Editions, 2014), which was nominated for an IndieFab Book of the Year Award. Melissa is the author of two poetry chapbooks: *The Pretty Machine* (ELJ Editions, 2017) and *The Karma Machine* (YellowJacket Press, 2011), which received the Peter Meinke Award. Melissa received her MFA from University of South Florida. She currently leads yoga trainings, retreats, and online workshops that weave mindfulness, creativity, and the power of narrative. Read more at www.TheYogaWriter.com.

Contents

All the Names for Goddess 17

Half Heart 18

String Theory 20

Dear Hungers 21

Calf Moon Prayer 23

I Want to Tell You Your Body Is Magic 24

7 Ways to Fake an Orgasm 26

The Mechanics of Sound 27

Rage 29

Straight to Hell 30

How to Cook Like an Italian Woman 32

Stolen Girls 34

To Speak to the Dead 36

Sequential 37

Music Is Measured in Small Marks 39

Swiss Women Upset The Time-Space Continuum 41

The Vaudeville Pussy, 1897 42

Your Orgasm as a Veritable Carmen Sandiego (I) 43

How to Hunt Down Your Orgasm, Guised as Carmen Sandiego (II) ... 44

Mating Habits of the Austro-Papuan Bowerbird 45

The Geminids 46

Seed 47

I Love the Girls 49

On Seeing the Girl in the River 50

Mandala 52

Occam's Razor 53

Panning for Stars 54

This Is Not an Elegy for Young Girls Who Dance 55

Bad Gods	56
Thermodynamics	57
Cantina	58
Beware the Poem with Wine Stain	59
Education at Hooters	60
The Pretty Machine	61
There Is No Tomorrow for This	63
Buddha Looks at a Glass	65
The Merits of Failure	66
Darkness Herself	67
Churning of the Ocean of Milk	68
Annica	70
On the Last Night of the World	71
Notes	73
Poems to Move to: A Yoga Index	75

"Their laughter rang out more holy than church bells."
— Susan Deer Cloud

All The Names For Goddess

I
Root-branch and mud-boot,
cracked seedpod sprayed
across dark earth. Venom
and calloused palms,
rain, bud, sugar, blade —
speak her names
and she will throw herself
from your tongue like a gift.

II
Her given language: root ripped from soil
and scream, blossom of blood, sigh,
every sound a verb, every song
a prayer.

III
When I say *woman* I mean *shakti*,
when I say *laughter* I don't mean polite
I mean jaw cracked wide to swallow the whole sky,
when I say *chakra* I don't mean wheel
I mean whirlpool, the churning of the ocean
of milk. In our galaxy nothing
is fixed, finite. There are goddesses
in every neighborhood. Watch for her
in her old coats; she is cutting
limes now, she is checking you out
at the gas station. Watch
as she draws blood from a needle, drives cattle
through snow, dodges ammunition
and breathes smoke.

IV
She does not need words to speak
the secrets buried in the dirt.
Her hands know the way, her feet are the garden
from which the world grows.
This is only one prayer,
and there are 10,000 ways to pray.

Half Heart

Each month new skin wraps around you
    dermal cells — a slick
        coat. Every four months
red blood cells flush veins and your bones
are rebuilding like roadwork all the time:
    osteocytes jackhammer the highways of your limbs
tibia and acetabulum re-gleamed as freshly paved asphalt.

Remarkable machinery! No wonder Walt Whitman
    couldn't contain himself. In a decade you've got all new bones
in fifteen years new muscles will braid your body pink —

How is it then shame still lives
    in my left hip the old curses
    still sing in my throat?

I sense those sixth-grade insults in my breasts
    like mold spores growing in a petri dish

can call up that freshman cigarette stench
    and nausea while I rode in Kelly Zabriski's backseat

and still the kindergarten trespass of my body
    during school assembly those fingers
that electrified me made maps of me
    and for all my brand new skin

the story is written beyond bone and blood cell and I'm afraid
    I will never find the first phrase I'm afraid
I can never — still. Still, some things stay
    with you your whole life: half your heart
for instance. Half your heart immutable
as a golden Buddha from the moment you were born

      it will not change   until you die —   so I'll take my half-heart
       like a small bird   in my nest of ribs   as they break down
     and re-skein   year   to year.   Even with
     immutable science   I still want to believe   some things
          last forever   and some things   never happened,
                          half of every heart   untouched.

String Theory

"The most cherished goal in physics, as in bad romance novels, is unification."
—Lee Smolin, theoretical physicist

Crank the star-making machine,
the universe gives birth again.
Brahma's eye cracks open
and a violin note splinters space
like a single bayonet, sprays sound
waves into matter, breath by breath by breath.
Tectonics lattice rock — the reverb *Om Namah* —
and mountains uplift. Next the violin strings
are stretched along latitudes, weaving metallic veins
across the globe until the dirt shrieks,
Brahma's bow scraping A sharp,
entire horizon wrapped in chords. The pulled strings
cast notes into fresh seafoam; the fission of this
dove-sound sends lichens soaring through
the wind and song becomes city, cloud
welcomes sky, mind meets desire.
Such brief music, and now here
we are slumped on old lawn chairs
with a pack of stale smokes and handful
of poems, and Lee Smolin, that old dog
whispering *I still had a small chance*
to discover something
because nature is much smarter
than all of us.

Dear Hungers

Rise to a boil. Bubble in your casks
and drift to air, gasping one last rebuke
at my open palms. Morning
is the closest promise. I stoke a fire

in my bones, turn myself
to smoke. In the swamps
and cypress marshes I welcome myself anew,
knowing the old girl

with sadness in her throat
can spit and boil, so I light myself
like soothsayer's incense, pray
to new and unknown gods. Pray

to Loddy, great aunt who threw
herself down five flights
of her Brooklyn row home — her husband found her
pills hidden, unswallowed. Now she becomes

my patron saint of coffee and cigarettes
on the stoop, patron saint of the olive green fridge,
patron saint of words dissolving
on a roof in New York. My hands are cups

brimming with questions
the dead keep —
they hand us nothing, only smoke
signals, straw dogs, static in the walls

which we interpret
for truth. Mystery
more holy than knowledge. *Tell me* —
what is more holy than grief?

The hungry ghosts clatter their demands
in the echoed cathedral
of my chest. I inhale, open my mouth, and let them rise
through me like curses, like hymnals.

CALF MOON PRAYER
After Derrick Austin

Love in the palms, the green spokes, the calloused hands. Love
in river mud and the veins that river in me, love written
by blood and silt and carbon. Love sits
between my eyes and the pit
of my belly. Forgive my sharp breaths,
my shut throat. Like the young calf
curled in the field by its mother, startled awake
in moonlight. The wind and flies tremble
russet fur. Like the night-blooming cereus, a wild spiked thing

that unfurls itself to darkness. Like a hand outstretched,
single flower opens its many-petaled palm. Like children
who ride their bikes and lift their hands off the handle bars —
only wanting to touch and be touched by air.

To spread like water.
Love in the cereus, who blooms one night a year
then becomes earth, becomes mayfly, yellow jacket,
jacaranda, bull calf, child. All water is working its way
back to the sea. Will you open your arms
to me like two great rivers? Will you open
the fragrant flowers of your palms?

I Want To Tell You Your Body Is Magic

I
Press one palm into the other. These hands are shale,
      these fine-grained bones. Warmth builds
in the shadowy slopes where fingers connect
          through a cushion of flesh, small landscapes. How strange
to feel your own hands — like tasting your own tongue — impossible.
Ligaments stretched like canvas sails,
      electrical sparks, fat like sheets
of insulation — my hands are filled with sibilance.
      Now I salivate a little. Need is a word
heavy as a stone. What does the body need?

II
This body has been a weapon, an invitation,
a canvas, a carving block, a bower.
This body has been taken, given. This body has been apology, sacrament,
punchline, middle finger, human-maker, murderer, open palm, fist.
      Need is a word heavy as a stone. What does the body need?

III
I want to tell you your body
      is magic. Your body deserves confetti cannons, pyrotechnics,
a goddamn drumline down 32nd Street. Even mine:
cell death and bloom, ordinary miracle
      of breath *in* and *out*
      a wing flapping
      in the chest and channel
of throat, all songs and unsaid words caught in the web
at the back of my mouth, my grit mouth, my ripening mouth,
my roof-scratched mouth, my startled mouth, my spell-casting mouth, my
dangerous mouth, my roiling mouth, my cursed mouth, my opaque mouth,
my sour tongue mouth, my luscious mouth, my pulsing mouth,
my voracious mouth, my timid mouth, my lyric mouth, my blessed mouth,
my singing mouth with jaw wide open and hungry
for air clean and sunbright
and in these gulps I am satisfied.

IV
They say white light.
They say your life unspools before you.
They say a parent or a saint will offer a palm from the other side.
Bring your finest gold, your glittering stones.
They say two coins to cross the river.
They say donate your liver, your lungs, your eyes. They say you will be judged.
They say Dimethyltryptamine, all power surge and punch in your brain,
a final supernova will shock you
light-bolt awake
so while you're here, hold
this, feel its blunt weight. Need is a word heavy
as a stone.

7 Ways To Fake An Orgasm

Obligatory, a quick convulsion
of grunt and grit teeth, or your breath

the thin thread holding the whole globe together.
There's the *orgasma melancholique* where memory recovers

a previous lover, one who knew the terrain
of your body like a carpenter knows the texture of trees,

like Jesus, which brings us
to the religious orgasm in which God is invoked,

a series of chants bearing his name. The pity orgasm
signifies he can jack-hammer away

ego preserved neatly intact. The orgasm of passion —
however malingered — is for the special one

who deserves a winning smile, a fantastic hair flip, a yelp
of ecstasy — an echo, perhaps, of that original groan

the lover's *Om* that struck the world into being.
The seventh usually occurs the first, awkward and sweating

against flannel sheets in his little brother's room
while his parents are visiting the Hoover Dam.

The seventh requires no fanfare, no burn.
Just a tap on the head

while he's rummaging around down there
and a simple, high pitched, *fin* —

whether he believes you or not
is another poem entirely.

The Mechanics Of Sound

I
The ears are everything: the eyes deceive,
the mouth explodes, the skin cringes
and the nose I chopped off years ago.
But the ears, they catch it all.

They go to work when other senses fail,
perking up at the slightest disturbance:
a sudden dip in altitude, in conversation,
a gather of bamboo staffs crackling in the breeze. Small things
worth noticing. The rest of reality dilutes and distorts,

but the ears cannot be fooled. They resonate to the vibration
of deeper sanctuaries. Like your breath echoing in the belly
of a glass bottle, Buddhists believe Om struck the world
into being, a giant violin string plucked,
a planetary hymnal, the whole globe
shaking softly.

II
When we die audio is the last to go —
each note a winged anthem,
a cell in the body.

III
My friend says when he drinks he can hear other spheres
rise up — voices of those long passed
pound on the ears of the drunk and listening, those
with unsaid wounds to lick.

III
Once I caught whispers in a breezeway,
sat long enough to hear the rustle
of a duck's beak through tall grass.
Small symphonies in palm fronds, floorboards.

IV
This Brooklyn cocktail singes my throat
which is good 'cause I don't want to talk.
On a stiff couch I sip and listen to a woman spout
her sanctimonious noise.
A buzzing creeps in my left ear, which I've heard
is the way angels communicate with mystics,
but I'm no mystic,
so it must be the gin.

Rage

On my altar I place three bones
from three boys: wrapped delicately
in cloth, so they believe I'm being tender. I tell them
hush, hush. I just want to touch. My hands are strong, don't you trust
me? Here I might lick my teeth.

My altar is nothing special: a low table, cracked wood. Dead flowers.
Ancient songs carved in legs.

Slowly I caress one wrist bone, the lunate — and whisper
if you tell anyone I'll say you're lying. You'll be sorry,
like a bad spell.

Dizzy I drink my own potion and believe I was right
to snap and clean and keep these bones for my own
pleasure — no harm if I take a little piece of you, right boys?
And they believe me, so primal is my tongue. They go on
with their small hollows, a little ghost piece here or there.
Who could tell? The lunate bone so tiny no one
would realize how it bridges hand to arm,
consequential pebble in the constellate body.
Small star, unknown and necessary, all mine.

Now ask me what I regret.

Straight To Hell

Eight years old and stuffed into white taffeta,
a cheap tiara dug my ripe skull.
At Our Lady Star of the Sea Church
I followed a procession of girls in white dresses

to the altar — we looked like a convoy of puff pastries.
Our patent leather shoes pressed the blood-colored carpet,
tulle and tiny rayon veils, fake pearls stitched to our socks,
all pomp and circumstance for Christ, who hung bare

on the cross along the wall. I'd heard I'd have to eat Him
from Father Spinaldo's golden cup, drink His blood from the chalice.
Christ looked thin and stale cut in wafers. One by one
the pastries opened their pink, plump mouths
and Father Spinaldo put Christ on their tongues,

the gift part of their own bones now, His body
on their breath. I wanted to swallow
salvation whole, I wanted
the mysterious world in me. I wanted

to do what adults did in mass each Sunday, eating Jesus,
to be part of His inner sanctum. But I couldn't
stomach Father Spinaldo's wrinkled hands reaching inside
my mouth, so I opted for the less direct method of holiness

and opened my palms. The wafer came down
from the cup and my fingers wavered — I dropped the Lord
on the carpet, panicked and kicked Him
under the choir's pew. Luckily Father Spinaldo

was busy offering Christ to the next girl in line,
so I marched to my seat, pretending to chew.
This sin was just as bad as lying in church, I was sure,
and guilt soaked through me

like olive oil into bread. Suddenly I knew
what kind of girl I'd be. My fate
sealed as the choir bloomed
into rolling hallelujahs.

How To Cook Like An Italian Woman

I
Of garlic clove, of white sheaths
peeled off the curved bulb, of knife slice
and sticky fingertips that mince
the cut white moons
to tiny broken teeth
for the cutting board.

II
Grandma Lola said no matter how poor we were
the secret was in the sauce: onion, oregano, single bay leaf
like a sinking flag. Sauce simmers with voices rising like steam,
spilling all over the house.

III
Their hands are not sparrows.
Italian women are orchestra conductors playing *appassionato*,
always moving. Their hands know verbs like *scrub* and *stir*
and *fix*, their songs are the rip of crusty bread
and the hum of *mmmm*,
that vibration, that heat
that fills your mouth.

IV
If an Italian woman is speaking in Brooklyn
she may be heard in Staten Island.
If three or more Italian women have gathered
you can eavesdrop in Bayonne. Beneath the glottis
boom and vault there is a love
that both craves and gives, there is a hunger
when she says the names of her children,
as if each of them were called loneliness.

V
Her voice carries these names, this one name,
out the kitchen window,
        she watches, my mother,
each of my syllables disappear
into the sky, and her eyes follow,
this moment she allows herself
then turns to the stove before
the water boils over.

Stolen Girls

Her face half scraped off
the sticker, her half eye glints
from pump #1 while I fill my tank.
For once the Florida light
isn't boiling at the edges. For once the clip sticks
on the first try, gas pours. The shredded letters
on the sticker: ABDUCTED
and I can't read anything else or make
out what she looked like, as if that mattered.
Imprint echoes in the summer fog,
gas stench gurgling from the pumps:
she is probably dead. I hold the thought
like a stone I'm not strong enough
to carry. Yesterday my friend,
a woman named after the moon,
was on her evening walk when an arm
wrenched around her throat,
sudden choke-gasp and spit-quick
thought: *This is real.*   But she's tough,
this moon-skinned mother-daughter:
as her vision blurred she swung and swung
hard and he released, ran. *So close
to being stolen*, she tells me, *but I still love
the world.* Later, she said she didn't, couldn't.
Love it. A man has been following me
at a public park: he sits in the grass,
drinks from tiny plastic liquor bottles, watches me.
I keep mace and a quartz crystal in my purse
for protection; my bases covered in all realms,
both here and there. The truth is
I'm scared. The gas station TV drones
and the pump thuds off. There is talk of angels
in the world. But we are talking of cells, syphoned
from the singular and made
increasingly complex. My cells

no different than the stolen girls'.
The angels are fast asleep. It is the gods
who should be most afraid now:
If no one believes in them anymore,
what power can they have?

To Speak To The Dead

face west. Your hands
may be full of stones, or they may be empty. Notice
how a cloud empties itself of itself,
its fruition a falling,

though that wasn't part of the plan — I bet it dreamed
of cirrus, asperitas, some new strata of cold sky
beckoning as any bright desire. Desire: not
a dirty word. As fire

consumes itself with its own glowing wounds.
We never foreshadow our becoming
until we're caught in the slip-slide
out from our own skin, pouring ourselves clean to air

or cindered and smoked
and by then it's too late to tell the others
the freedom of how the formless
move through space, unstitched from the fabric
of time, more luminous than sun, more thunderous
than storm, more arrival than departure, at last.

Sequential

"We live 100 years, but suppose we lived a billion years. A stone would be just a moment in which some sand gets together and then it disaggregates, so it's just a momentary getting- together of sand."

~ *Carlo Rovelli, physicist*

Fleck the glass, spin it and stack it
like translucent bricks
to build the past, memory's cracked

prism. Time is a poem
cut up into minutes, definable
things. Set your offerings on the altar

of nouns — only that which you name
is real. Call it what you call it,
and it bows beneath its letters:

the *good old days* get better
in a flawed calendar, the alien
edged in darkness, the slut who is not

your daughter waits in the clinic.
A word is a reality, and deep in the breathing
Amazon, the Amondawa don't have a word

for time — snipped free of the past, no dread
for the future, even age isn't counted
but stages of life are symboled: the toddler shrugs off

her toddler name when her baby brother grows up
to claim it for a while. No language map
links space to clock. They are a happening,
a whirlpool made of new water
in the orbit of day and night where
they will never say they don't have enough time —

uncommodified, clean pane of glass. But even the timeless
won't last forever: the scientists slip Portuguese
onto Amondawa tongues and slowly time erects itself

around days, months, decades — a dwelling spot
like a clot in the brain, now irrefutable
as stone. With every new sentence

the ancient words go extinct.
Every noun is a lie, while the real
rises and swarms and slides downstream.

Music Is Measured In Small Marks

Who's to say desire won't outlive us?
—Helen Wallace

When someone falls in love, a giant toothed wheel
clicks on and hooks the earth's axis,

tugging all 7 billion of us
on a slightly different angle,

so imperceptible no one has yet
to notice, not even NASA. Though

maybe the gypsy women notice,
those whose hands tremble in dry heat

as they cross over ley lines,
Machu Picchu and Sedona mesa.

Cosmic switches flick underground,
upsurge to their mottled palms.

These women taste possibility
in the air and it tastes like lemongrass.

Their nostrils flare. Because someone's in love
somewhere in the world, light is growling

through these windows. Because someone's in love,
the river is running

on watered down wine,
the river is shallow and shoal-filled.

Because despite every reason not to,
some people still hunker down

into that rifting space
for bone and flesh

where every sigh is measured as music
in small marks on the staff.

Some say the earth is singing —
rippling sound into space, a pitch

that tastes of lemon
and the sweat on the back

of your lover's neck. This planetary song, all vibrato
and string pluck, rings too in our molecules, little songs,

sonnets in our teeth, in the fingertips we use
to trace lines across one another's bodies

knowing music as the mouth's open curve,
resounding, and infinite.

Swiss Women Upset The Time-Space Continuum

As for the immutable laws of the universe,
certain women have found loopholes.

There are many methodologies: sequin corsets, knives,
gels designed in Swiss labs by chemists

all named Alise. In steel corridors, legions
of 6-foot women upset the time-space continuum,

here beauty is inspected like a malarial mosquito. The Alises
are doing very important work. Around the world, the good people

are grateful for possibility aglow on glassy counters, for the arrow of time
flipped on its back. The Alises help people scour happiness

on their skins for small fortunes. All day in white lab coats
these women see particles explode

in shimmering gasps. Bent over microscopes, they consider
the tiniest particulars in slender test tubes,

they decode the seductive math.
The Alises watch cells burst

into plumes of beauty,
life flickers iridescent fire

and what they don't tell us
but still what we know: how each cell

dies out eventually, each light
at intervals flicks off. How darkness blooms

over a body and becomes
husk, symbol, straw dog,

a desperate map with no
guiding constellation, no fixed star.

The Vaudeville Pussy, 1897

Lona, Sophia, Inger, Olga, Gertrude —
even their names sound like the scratch
and ruffle of tulle skirts, fake silks
shining beneath stage lights at Koster & Bial's

New York City Concert Hall. Those five Danish blondes
called their act The Wickedest Girls in the World.
I imagine Lona, the oldest — with theatre training
back in Copenhagen — bosses her flurry of sisters
as talcum powder mushroom-clouds the dressing room

before the girls spin onstage
and sing the "Nazi, Nazi Song":
Who wears a golden monogram on the buttons
of his pants? And some dainty little pet will put himself in debt?
Dos ist der Nazi, Ein Nazi yoder kant, in seiner art gauz excellent.

This, friends, is not the number the gals were known for.
Their shocker, their coup de grace, when the sisters lift their skirts
knee-high and ask the crowd, *Do you want to see my pussy?*
and the crowd starts to sweat a little under the arms
and behind the knees. The men in the back swirl their dark liquor
coolly, the men in front yell *Yes! Dear God Yes!*
and the girls hike their hems to each unmask
hand-sewn underwear with a live kitten
fastened to the front.

What was it like for those five kittens, cloaked and roasting
beneath spotlights and tulle, smelling of sweat and rose oil?
Can you almost hear their terrified mews?
I imagine Gertrude, the youngest and arguably most talented,
doesn't like the pussy routine and glides smoother during shenae turns;
between numbers she softly reassures the cat strapped
to her pubic bone, rubs its greasy head with her thumb. Gertrude knows
about heat in the belly. Her songs are brief salves
for the animal body, a chance to shake off shame
like wet fur. With a wink she says
we're here just a short while, let's delight
in ourselves.

Your Orgasm As A Veritable Carmen Sandiego (I)

Slippery, isn't she? A swift red flick
of the flesh and then — *poof* —
she's slid off to Buenos Aires or Katmandu,
wherever it is your shimmer crests
once she leaves the light-swallowed bed.

That specter, fever-quick thrash, spent.

Imagine her in her wide-brimmed hat, exploring
great cities, sipping tea, reading her horoscope (Scorpio, obviously).
Imagine she sets fire to everything she touches.
> The Mekong Delta, le Arc de Triomphe, and all of Manhattan
> will go down in one ecstatic cry.
> Newspapers will say it was an earthquake,
> but you'll know the source of such blood-fruit eruptions.

You lie naked in bed, tempted
to jump out your lover's window and hunt down your orgasm,
guided magnetic to your rightful thrush.
But stay. The sheets feel cool
all of a sudden.
Steep yourself inside this moment, suspended
between fever and peace — perhaps
it will bring you one step closer
to enlightenment. Hold this longing like a stone
in your palm. Know something
of loss, feel
its emptiness and
its weight.

How To Hunt Down Your Orgasm, Guised as Carmen Sandiego (II)

Say you don't stay in bed — you refuse to lie there limp-limbed,
leeched of fever. You've known too many kinds of loss
to let this one slip away, so you jump
naked out your lover's window down two stories,
clutching the bed sheet as a parachute.

Ravenous you, desperate-panting you
search down city streets and crowded shopping malls —
      (your bed sheet now doubles as a toga)
      strangers will smile, understanding. They'll remember
      that first time when they were young
      and felt the slick quake between their legs,
      small blue spindles, strange and a little queasy.
      Afterward their eyes darted around rooms —
      did anyone notice the great rift in them,
      the demarcation of their lives
      as pre-orgasm and post?
      Oh yes, they'll understand the trouble you're in.

And when you finally do catch her in a café (red hat hiding one eye)
you touch her sparkling light,
get your brief detonation: frayed wires switch up
your thighs, bones snap off your spine one by one,
a great clatter down the sidewalk, falling
entirely apart, which everyone knows
is the only way to be put back together.

Mating Habits of the Austro-Papuan Bowerbird

Consider the jumping spider:
        the females are bland as chestnuts
but the males, now — they are all white speckles,
        tangerine legs, hairs contouring the eyes
        in the most splendid shapes. Oh,
        to be an ugly lady jumping
spider and have my pick of the pack
as the handsomest ones claw
        each other for my eggs.
Or why not be a green tree frog and listen
        as the males crank their lonely throat-calls into the night?
It would be like that movie *Say Anything*, where John Cusack
        holds up the huge boom box to serenade the girl,
except it would be hundreds of John Cusacks
        huddled together, blasting their love songs
        to sire me.

Consider the bowerbird who builds his courtship stage
        on a golf course in Australia. Tucked behind the ninth hole
he is busy arranging meticulous twigs painted in plant juices,
        collecting treasures: snail shells, beetle wings, broken plastic bottles.
He dances up and down
        his grass promenade, all flash and blue feather
        while a foursome in pink polos and khakis swing and curse and swig
        cold beer, tireless pantomime and pushpins
in the gut — who can say what is precious, what is charade?
        Whose hour more worthy? I imagine the female bird
nearby in her enclave of vine tendrils
        and splintered leaf-light. She is alone and lacking pity,
        glittering eyes wet and alive.

The Geminids

      Each year the waters wind their clocks toward the center
of the sea, and there
      a table is set.

By December we plunge sunward
      through a meteor net,
our tiny planet swinging deftly past the burning stones

      that clip my stomach each time I see one and feel gilded
by something so far and indifferent
      from me. The instant keeps me like a locket.

I drive north
      where the sky is a thick fleece
over the neighborhood. My father left the lamp hot

      in the living room and handed me his coat. He stayed
up until midnight, showed me the hill
      and the dark theater to the east

rimmed with slash pines and sabal palms.
      I lay in the cold grass while the wind talked
through leaves as if afraid of itself

      and light years away
debris danced; the sky dripped
      with another flash of light.

Seed

Bright blood-grain on paper, she cuts
the seeds free, buries them
in black dirt and a brief salve
of darkness.

*

She is thirteen
and men are becoming cartographers
of her body and she is beginning
to realize this in a half haze
of nausea, half haze of validation.

*

So much hate can live
in the animal body;
a sentence got stuck in the crook
of her knee, another is looping
her neck. A rustling
of hands becomes part
of the breath pattern, words make cells
no matter how long buried,
and what is buried
can be born.

*

She is fourteen
and women are becoming cartographers
of her body and she understands
all life is relational: a breast is not
a breast, a body parsed can only be known
by other parts, through other's eyes.

*

By fifteen she's mapped
herself: cruel inheritance.
Worth is an equation she works
at constantly.

*

Seeds are metaphors, yes,
but they are metaphors for even
themselves: big-bang pinprick,
subatomic spark, imagine all the universe
condensed to the faint pause before breath, expulsion —

I Love The Girls

who wear skin like wet leaves,
light plinking on the slopes
of their upper lips.

I love the live oak girls
with plaited hair, stone faced
as they haul ex lovers' upright pianos
out third story windows.
I love the girls who wind chokers
around throats with charms
dangling to ridged collarbones.

I love the space-age girls in foil uniforms
who float the stratosphere and eat dehydrated
ice cream. I love the wax girls
encased behind museum glass,
the ones who haven't moved
for years though their glass eyes boil.

I love the girls who ride the El Train
to Brooklyn Heights, past metal push
cart vendors racked with headlines
and candy wrappers, the girls who listen
to iPhones and the girls who don't, the girls
who sling purses around shadow-cast
shoulders, whose eyes flash beneath rushing
underground lights.

I love these girls of air and marrow and sinew
straight clipped to the teeth, blood spinning
wildly as my own, our rivers running
into our seas, the ancient hymns of our mothers
at the banks.

I love the girls who dunk their heads
below the surface of Horseshoe Lake,
slicked hair purpling down their backs,
skin shining like wet leaves.

On Seeing The Girl In The River

Maybe she made love that morning
or sliced her hand cutting mango and lifted
a blood-thumb to lips, sucked the wound shut.
The bright sky wordless — as if
between taking breaths — then

deep rumble, sudden snap of wood
and bone, a father's
scream, a chorus screaming,
the whole world
                tipped up as water like a jet liner
        swallowed streets and porticos crumbled, mud streamed and stained
            clothes-skin-air-tongue-back of tongue-farther,
roofs ripped off homes
            like hats, thrashed
    in dark surf along
a thousand empty shoes, those lost boats.

The sea veins gushed, punishing
fault lines and flat lines but no
warning system in that ocean, no
prophecy for its epicenter, pulse and madness —

then silence, then lotus petals above her head, weightless.

Two days later she bobs
face down with the now limp breeze
swaying palms and arms
    listless like driftwood
indifferent to the water spiders
navigating her ankles and neck.

On the riverbed, before her body is hauled up
a photographer sets to work, but her pants are torn at her rear end
    exposing a black layer of underwear, and as he shoots

I want to run to her, black water splashing,
I want to cover her with my arms, shield her
from her final photo with her pants split. I want to fold my body
        over hers, tell her it's ok,
but I am reminded of the foolish things the living say
and the dead already know.

Mandala
After the Sacred Art Tour of Tibetan Monks in the United States

Their robes purl around them
        like spilled turmeric —
Tibetan monks shimmy bright
        sand grains through chak-pur
with the *sshck-sshck* of each stroke
        as the wheel of dharma cranks another round
        and the sun slides below

the low-lying city. We squeeze ourselves
        in the art gallery for a closer view
of the sacred circle. The air shut off to still the sand
        we sweat in our coats. No one exhales. On the mandala's outer rim
flames sweep westward, blue winds swirl.
        A pink lotus blossoms. On the inner rim a cross, a crescent, star
        of David, hand of Fatima,

meticulous strokes — slowly the world is built
        from the tiniest grain. Tomorrow
the monks will sweep the mandala
        back to bright chaos,
march downtown and dump it in the bay
        with a blessing for world peace. Could we march ourselves to the edge
        and open our palms, could we let the world slip through our fingers
in the gesture of receiving, the gesture of release?

Occam's Razor

The imagination is a terrible machine.
In a single hour I've created you killed,

bludgeoned by the manager of a seedy Japanese spa
or ejected from your drunk friend's windshield, the night

swallowing you whole. Or maybe you're lying in the Elysian field
of a busty gal's mattress, the blonde at the bar who laughed too loudly

at your jokes, so you smiled and bought vodka
to numb both your tannic skins.

By hour four in my apartment I should remember Occam's Razor,
that you're probably passed out on someone's couch

and you'll call tomorrow intact. But my brain
flits against Occam's predictable cosmos,

certain the universe deals in knives
and poison darts, certain

something dark and delicious
has surely befallen you.

Panning For Stars

We sit on the curb and sip convenience store wine
watching stars cartwheel above. I talk too much
while you throw cigarettes
at disinterested pigeons. On the cusp
of daybreak we are lucky in the wake
of space time, fingers stamped with tar
and horizon. Distant galaxies streak the sky, smoke-like,
all possibility dimmed in this half-morning, all longing
drowned in cheap shiraz.

And when you walk away it isn't me trailing you,
or my voice pressing your back asking *what of all this?*
It's only the moon, bald and indifferent.

A string of lights, not a metaphor, reaches
my apartment to yours across 17th Street.
Your balcony now empty, the broken
green lawn chair and a pot
of ungrown basil on the sill.

It could drive me to madness and more shiraz, but there
is something like love hidden
in the concrete groves, there is something
like love burning all the houses down
on this street. There just might be
love up there, sifting stars
like chunks of gold high above
the crumbling rooftops, far beyond
the pigeons' sickly coos, where we are forgiven
our tempest words, where
we are forgiven everything.

This Is Not An Elegy For Young Girls Who Dance

Sara Ciccone, do you remember
how we pulled white and gold feather boas
from your dress-up chest and slung them over
our shoulders, how they frothed our skins like steamed
milk? How we posed at your mother's gold-flocked
mirror and danced to Madonna — we were
eight in '92 — we were kindling, waiting
to be smoked. You said you were Madonna's
niece — big-boned in Mom's Revlon, trying on
glamour because we'd been taught to. Though we
didn't yet speak the word *sexy* we felt
it plush as red velvet, as black satin
tongue. Did you lie about your famous aunt?
All little girls lie. Everyone knows this.

Bad Gods

They have been gods in their meager
bones, born of no pure favor. They
have been able to throw words
like ammunition, arms like ammunition,
ammunition like ammunition

and because
even gods with bad breath
and bounced checks and cancer growing
like a secret in their prostate are beyond
consequence, with their eyes these men
have scraped and pawed, with their paws
they have scraped and taken, and my body, my complicit body

was another battleground and my voice, my voice loud
as a leather belt with a laugh that cracks my jaw suddenly
flew off. The singing bird in my throat
gone. Is it because love

is made complicated, and I wanted
to be loved?
They thought
it was their right
and my role, their eyes
like heat lamps, their wounds
like folded notes I am only now
learning how to read, each letter
burning as I open my mouth
and speak.

Thermodynamics
for Monica

Our bodies are white hot light
spun from distant stars, construed
as skin and bone and pulse. This
is not to be romantic, or dramatic,
but the hard-edged surface of some kind
of truth, an arrowhead
that doesn't soften because cutting is unpleasant,
it merely cuts through. There is the old song,
one minute you're here, the next you're gone. And
yet you're also still here:
electrons in new orbit, that light not left, still
very much swirling around all
that you love — the banyan leaves, her hair.

You are here, but we must call you different names
now: the wind that startles the trees awake,
that lifts her black hair from her face. We call you
bluejay, sunrise, cloudbank. What we have forgotten?
These could be, are, our names too —
this shared name written
in the singular unspoken language,
words finer than mist, sharper than truth.
You cannot hear it but you can feel it. My letters now clumsy,
too dense. Made of carbon and heat and stardust, such
a small piece of the world, useless
and necessary and sighing with starlight.

Cantina

Days on the road cut in all directions,
pulp an orange peel sky to pure madness — there's melody,

you wailing on the harmonica and me on the spoons,
the wondrous clattering sounds drown the clock ticks, make

the sun shake. You sing me songs of ancient wars
as we ride like we're running away but it's always toward.

Uncertainty is a half-written sentence. You say you're afraid
so we sweeten our tongues with agave nectar

but it doesn't keep me from swearing so much,
my mother would call me unladylike and say

what man will want you with a mouth like that.
We're in a roadside cantina between two Ponderosa pines

drinking tequila from tin cups
and scattering feed for chickens.

I'm thinking about these chickens, about soft necks slit
and fresh eggs cracked, about the sky

pressing its blue thumb on us, this wood shack carved
into another untethered afternoon, pretending

to be endless. The thought of all that possibility
sucks the air out of this wide field — as if in answer a thunderclap

chars the blue, splits a bolt southwest and suddenly
these chickens, the tequila, it's perfect.

I smile at you, lift my tin cup. It's true, *the world can't help
but reveal itself to us*. Red and white feathers and ripped open sky.

Beware The Poem With Wine Stain

Light halos my fingertips against the paper,
a poetry book in my hands. Glass on the table,
blood-bead of merlot at its base, that last undrinkable
bit. My love playing blues and DeBussy on his grandmother's upright
this late Friday night. Half-wilted spider mum in a hand-me-down vase, all
the trappings of a life I'd call rich and vicious
with happiness. And Lao Tzu in the back of my brain like a song
in the next room — *ever desireless, one sees the mystery,*
ever desiring, one sees only the manifestations. One foot

sucked deep in the mud, daily life calf-heavy; one foot suspended, held
like a half-smirk in the air. Non-grasping. Such a novice I am, and drunk
with love for the golden dusk, piano notes, this precious breath, please
just another line of poetry, one more tune, another sweet red sip.
There is never just one thing.

Dread threads happiness, how wine takes the shape
of its cup. How a hammer creates melody. Beware
the finger pointing at the moon, beware the poem
for blood-pulse, for life itself. You know

I don't believe that, either. The poem is pulse, not diagram —
haven't you, with your own fingertips
reached into the page, made halos
with words, stepped into the temple and touched
the holiest thing directly?
When you are afraid, aren't you also
sharply alive?

Education At Hooters

Plasticine goddesses in flesh-colored tights greet you with blinkless eyes: Kelsey or Leila or Chantalle lead you past day-glo lights strung over the bar, past neon waitresses sashaying in Lycra, whirling trays of 3 Mile Island hot wings and pitchers of beer, past men in football jerseys who yowl at TVs, past fraternity boys wielding laminated fake IDs like medals, past a middle-aged man at a table cracking jokes to a waitress who bounces her cleavage with each *ha* for a bigger tip, past the man's drunk wife in kitten heels with pink smeared lipstick careening to the bathroom as if on stilts — whose eyes slash at you under spider lashes and you catch the sadness in her, laced in beer foam, just for a moment, can't be sure — past their young son at the table who is now learning all the ways love moves.

The Pretty Machine

I
Break the mirrors, shear the wolves, pluck
the crimson posts from ears and stick them
in the riverbanks. Where rivers flow mouths
will open, and starving are the egos
at the filling station. The ego is tenacious; it hides
in high school cafeterias and shopping plazas,
in the sequined queens whose locust hair
and perfect white fangs deliver us from evil; it hides
on the meditation cushion one inch from enlightenment.

Pretty girls, watch those tanned, toned backs — not
for vengeful choir girls but for all the good
you never did. Anyone can wave a manicured palm
and wish for world peace, but the children
are still bloodied: say their names
through designer lip gloss.

II
When my best friend and I were ten we played for hours,
laughing wild little-girl laughs, unaware
that any day we'd learn to laugh
while trying to look thin, to laugh
and pose for anyone whom might be watching.

On the cusp of puberty our bodies still belonged to us,
when our games were simple and our hair was dirty.
If we weren't careful soon we'd be fed to the Pretty Machine,
like a wood chipper, arms and legs and brains
on the glittering conveyor belt.

We'd come out the other side as still-life paintings of ourselves,
shellacked and lacquered, shell-shocked
and pretty.

III
One day I chopped my nose off.
I say I did it for myself, but really it was for the boys
in fifth grade who called me Toucan. It's for the packed nerves
soldered in my throat,
how they sparked,
for the schoolmates' fingers folded around my locker room neck hissing
ugly girl die ugly girl die
which then became my heartbeat.

IV
The Pretty Machine sways
with circadian rhythms
where breast lifts and lip plates
and purging spells dance
beneath earth's fluorescent lights.

V
When mothers carve only love
into tectonic plates,
when girls run barefoot, hair tangled,
laughing unbroken, their bodies
belonging to them, then may we know
the ley lines
of a woman's heart.

There Is No Tomorrow For This

Slipped beneath the waves
wrapped in fog, cast gray
the news reports all said the Sewol listed, listed
but that word is a hiccup, its short *i* and lisp
of *s*, its blunted decrescendo.

The ferry carrying three-hundred twenty five
students did not list. It shot
like a gun through shallow water,
gray and steel and cold and
colder still. The children, the passengers
were told to remain calm, remain
in their seats. The Yellow Sea rose
to the windows

and eleven miles away there are the parents
breaking in a tent on the coast.
Their eyes bleach the horizon, their eyes
will never look away. When
the rescue teams were delayed
due to bad waters
one mother, whose sixteen-year-old son was missing,
screamed *there is no tomorrow for this.*

The listing, sinking ship
full of their children is buried
underwater. Sank, the word like an anvil

hitting sandbed, grains blossoming in the lucid
terrible sea bottom; sank, with its flat *a*
like an abrasion you don't fully feel at first,
a marrowed burn beneath the scrape that lasts
and never fully leaves you.

Another mother, huddled in the tent, said
I feel like we are here
waiting for our children
to die. A thoughtless wind blew down
the coast, lifted her hair, then left.

Buddha Looks At A Glass

and laughs, how lovely it shapes
                water, how light
passes through and shimmer emerges,
                how it may fall

from the shelf
        or catch a wayward elbow,
              hurtling to the floor.
He knows it may break
        and it's already broken,
              edged crystals yoked
        in smooth glass, imperceptible

to the eye. He lifts the cup to his lips,
        kisses the rim, water gives
              to his mouth.

Every breath
        a tender bone,
                a roomful of memory
        where we have each snapped apart
            and been yoked back

together. Our jaws unhinge,
        water spills from our tongues, flooding
                the streets.

The Merits Of Failure

A stone becomes unbidden
by the mountainslope, is loosed
and flings downward.

Watch any still scene
for long enough and it will come alive
on you: the mountain is, yes,
slipping back into the sea.
Close your eyes and listen
to the rocks trill down ledges, mercied
to the pull toward the center,
as we are all stumbling
to our own center, all held
in gravity's hands.

The air cracked with dry heat, hard earth.
And yet, when we tip
our heads to the sky, that indifferent roof,
our palms up in desperation, our mouths
in the pained curl of *why,*
we are also in the gesture
of accepting, the corners of our lips
drawn up, our trembling
hands open for a gift
we cannot yet possibly imagine.

Darkness Herself

Child of winter, crystalline bones.
    North mother of French tongue and fever,
        mother of summers with sky always burning — still
how she hates the sun.   Doesn't every child cling,
    then turn, then return   eventually?
    It may take more than one
        lifetime to come back
          to her arms. It may take more than one moon

to unbury my old spells,
    to dig up dark earth and allow myself
        to be surprised, to let darkness herself,
        ancient mother rise up from the fissures
          through soil, through loam —

darkness how long
    I have evaded you; lit everything
    that would catch, flicked every flashlight
        and turned myself to bonfire
    kept running   until breathless, smoke dripping
from my hair —all in
the name of what: fear?   The layer beneath the layer
where I would not look?   Yet here you are

    unshaken as a ghost. Your hands reach out
        like spilled oil   all gloss and night,
    and in your open palms a mirror,
        my face reflected.   In the wet of my eyes, my mother's.

Let the words lay themselves down. Let the old spells hush now.
    Fold in.   Dear darkness, teach me
        what you have to teach.

Churning Of The Ocean Of Milk

The gods have grown tired
and a little cranky.
They've been clanging cupboard doors
late nights, looking and looking again
for something they can't seem to find.
They open the fridge, then shut it.
Their meditations are ragged
with anger.

The ancients called it *amrita*, honeyed
droplet. Every story has its nectar,
everybody's got a want — even Buddha
sought nirvana. And Vishnu, blue-skinned

and sweet-faced atop his lotus
tells the gods the one thing
they don't want to hear: *Go to the demons
because you can't do this alone.*

They frown and suggest heading to town for a pint:
demons are older than gods,
made of the same carbon and moonlight,
made of seedlings,
despite their brash talk and blood-stained teeth.
Together they churn the ocean of milk,
where every word is an echo, every metaphor
a leap, so think cosmic, think Milky Way —
who isn't seeking immortality, anyway?

The galaxy swirls for thousands of years,
heliotropics and pink-cloud nebulae
glitter god eyes and demon eyes — finally
at the center someone spots a geyser,
but not nectar. A flume of gas, green stench
that chars throats: gods and demons
hunch over, dry heaving. Poison rises first (always first).

Who wouldn't want to give up? Whirlpooling
the long stretches between dead stars, sweating and unsure
until a demon spots a gold bead —
amrita, finally, a flicker after all this time.
Taste sunlight, a cupful,

and who doesn't love a tale that ties itself up?
But this is just the beginning: a galaxy spirals,
a thought latches, a hand grasps. The thing
we're seeking never saves us,
only makes us new.

Anicca

"Better it is to live one day seeing the rise and fall of things than to live a hundred years without ever seeing the rise and fall of things."
~ Buddha

Season of blackberry, season of hooked thorn, season of striated sky;
calving season, of blooms split off leaves and pollen hanging in heat
like unsaid wounds. Season of cirrus then season of cloud glut,
season of slow evening rains. Season of hustle, season of fever, season
of talking too much. Season of fly hatch and lizard egg, season of dragonflies
cutting the lower sky; season of locust, season of frog song.
Season of tilling and seeding and waiting. Season of easy mornings,
two eggs in the skillet, season for poems and honey. Season of purge
and scour, season of burn piles and meteor showers.
Season of harvest, season of burial.
Season of dusk and early darkness. Season of quiet, cold.
Season of music, neon, tonic, pyrite. Season of mud boot
and firefly. Season of drought, then floods,
the cypress stands submerged then sucked dry
in keen circles round the sun. Now,
this very day, the lettuce
yelps out of dirt and spirals skyward
until its flowered breath exhales,
its leaves turn bitter. This very day
we take our shovels to bury the stillborn calf, red fur slick
with afterbirth, blue eyes full
of clouds — we hoist her by her small hooves
to the ditch we dug
near the shade of a live oak, our silence
sacrament while in the next pasture
a young calf watches, blinks, chews cud
in the sun. By next season today's sadness
will give way like topsoil to some unforeseen joy,
some slant of light, some greater pain
come round to take its place.

On The Last Night Of The World

darkness warps around the fire dancer,
    her lit hoops swirl over and over on the axis
of her hips, tides pulled by her thighs
    where stars lie hidden, succulent fruit.

We are thick in the field, peach juice pinking and sticky
    down our chins, we drown our mouths
in sweetness this night.
    Only sweet words left to speak — what else is there to say? All the guns

lie barely cold. We emptied tunnels
    into one another,
we finger the holes rusting in our loved ones' breasts,
    the cleared smoke not yet made ghost.

We do not cry because there is no need. We are readying ourselves
    for earth-rumble, for bone-snap,
the burst incandescent — a wild, magnificent thing
    and also a small flicker at the end

of the dark map.
    Soon snuffed out, forgotten experiment.
Except, perhaps, for the echo of our *I-love-yous*,
    for the memory of peach-sweet etched into cosmic fabric,

faintest ripple to the farthest corners, where someone or something
    may touch it and recoil — feel the hot bolt of hip-fire, otherworldly
of this night where once, long ago,
    legend goes we burned.

Notes

"On Seeing the Girl in the River" is in reference to the 2004 Indian Ocean Tsunami.

"There Is No Tomorrow for This" references the South Korean Ferry, the *Sewol*, which sank on April 16, 2014. Of the 476 people on board, 304 died during the tragedy. Most of the fatalities were high school students attending a school trip.

"Annica" is a Pali word for impermanence, which is central to the Buddhist tradition.

Poems to Move to: A Yoga Index

"Yoga is the poetry of the body."
    ~ Rodney Yee

The truth is that you live in a breathing, pulsing, visceral body. Language is an act of making our sensorial, phenomenal experience all the more real to us through the power of imagery, metaphor, and verbs. Every literary device is like an eager finger pointing us to something. Every word is a friend saying "Look! Look! Pay attention."

This Yoga Index is an invitation to embody some of the poems in this collection. Feel free to "strike a pose" and read the suggested poem pairings (some are more suited for reading during the posture, such as Padmasana/ Lotus Pose, while others are best read prior to entering the pose, such as the advanced Danurasana / Wheel Pose). Our hope is to bridge your reading experience from the solely cerebral dimension to the physical as well.

Note:
Please don't wrangle yourself into a posture if it's not appropriate for your body at this time. Contrary to popular belief, the point of yoga is not to get yourself into a pretzel shape. Even the Lotus Pose depicted is very advanced, and is not appriopriate for anyone with tender knees, tight hips, or a sensitive lower back (which is to say, most modern Americans): feel free to sit comfortably on the floor instead, with your hip bones slightly elevated on a pillow or cushion, so that your knees rest lower than your hips.

Padmasana / Lotus Pose

Pairs well with:

All the Names for Goddess (p. 17)
I Want to Tell You Your Body Is Magic (p. 24)

Balasana / Child's Pose

Pairs well with:

    Annica (p. 70)
    Darkness Herself (p. 67)

Ardha Hanumanasana / Half Split

Pairs well with:
> String Theory (p. 20)
> Music Is Measured in Small Marks (p. 39)

Parivrtta Virabhadrasana / Revolved Warrior

Pairs well with:

    Sequential (p. 37)
    The Churning of the Ocean of Milk (p. 68)

Vrksasana / Tree Pose

Pairs well with:

    Buddha Looks at a Glass (p. 65)
    The Geminids (p. 46)

Dhanurasana / Wheel Pose

Pairs well with:

    Mandala (p. 52)
    The Merits of Failure (p. 66)

www.ingramcontent.com/pod-product-compliance
Lightning Source LLC
Chambersburg PA
CBHW020702300426
44112CB00007B/485